Communicating Encouragement

A Quick Guide for Educators to Enhance Communication to Students and Parents to Maximize Learning Potential.

Dr. Alexandra V. Maragha

Communicating Encouragement

Alexandra V. Maragha

ISBN: 978-0-578-44974-6

Copyright © 2019 Alexandra V. Maragha

All rights reserved. No part of this book may be reproduced or transmitted in any form or by any means, electronic or mechanical, including photocopying, recording, or using any information storage and retrieval system, without the prior written permission of the publisher, except for including brief quotations in a review and other noncommercial uses permitted by copyright law.

To all of those who encouraged me and to all whom I encourage under the knowledge and power of One.

The Most Merciful, The Most Kind.

Contents

Introduction VII

ONE: Don't Teach, Talk! 1

TWO: Reveal the Truth –"Honesty *is* the Best Policy" 4

THREE: Progressive Positive Discussion (PPD) 6

FOUR: Repetition of Expectations 10

FIVE: *Be* the Encouragement! 13

Personal Contract for Encouragement 15

About the Author 17

Introduction

Communicating with students and parents is education's most obvious yet complex task. While most educators have a captivated student audience daily, the process of communicating learning is sometimes blocked for many reasons, resulting in poor student performance. One of the leading factors in poor student performance is the breakdown of overall encouragement. This can occur due to educators' lack of attention and understanding of how to encourage students and parents, as parents are also the third base in the "trifecta" relationship of learning in the K-12 system.

This book guides educators in communicating encouragement to students in classroom settings, one-on-one, and as a group, and communicating with parents about their children to encourage support for learning development at home.

Education is a demanding field, and the unexpected is ever-present. The attention that must always be placed on students can leave no time to answer a question from a co-worker or parent in passing. The basic tools learned in preparation, presentation, and performance can sometimes be lost in a moment of chaos. This book also serves as a reminder and a refreshed way to look at how to communicate with understanding and remove factors that may block the communicative learning process between educators, students, and parents.

I want to thank you, educators and parents, for the effort and encouragement you provide young minds, and I hope you continue to do so.

ONE: Don't Teach, Talk!

Timing is everything, especially when it comes to when to speak about what and how. Lecturing and giving formal instruction are most appropriate when introducing and teaching a topic. Talking to students and parents one-on-one should be done less formally and appropriately, according to the purpose. A formal lecture would not be appropriate if a student has a question during work time in class and approaches the instructor one-on-one. However, an adjusted way of speaking and talking with that student to understand their needs and encourage them to ask questions is better suited. Likewise, when speaking to parents one-on-one, the role of an educator is not to educate about a topic in general conversations (unless asked directly) but instead to inform and talk with them about their children's performance.

Teaching and lecturing, when one should simply be talking, can negatively impact how information is communicated. Such negative impacts can include:

- **Reverse Affect:** One will do the opposite when told to do something.
- **Nagging:** When someone is told something repeatedly over time, this can lead to the receiver " shutting down" and no longer paying attention to either **the request itself, the person making the request, or both.**

- **Lack of Clarity from Language:** Depending on students' grade level and subject matter, the language used formally to lecture or teach might not be understood in-depth by students and parents. This could be due to English being a second language or not spoken at all, the education level of parents, or the **home environment**.
- **Becoming Inapproachable:** When communicating formally at all times, students and parents may become less likely to approach for support or help.

Conversations further the two-way communication process, while traditional conferences are more one-way focused. Although synonymous, conferences are usually carried out as structured, formal, one-way presentations about a student's performance, with the parent receiving a message without much consideration for ongoing dialogue. Even if parents have questions at those times, many do not fully speak up about concerns based on a traditional parent-teacher conference environment. Many parents find this environment intimidating and fast-paced, as they don't feel they have enough time to discuss their concerns while other parents wait in line. Likewise, many educators fall into a script when talking to parents to ensure they complete everything required in the allotted time. Other environmental factors, such as parents or children walking around, a quick "hi" from someone passing, announcements, or just chatter noise, can distract parents and teachers. Such moments then can leave information that needs to be communicated by either the parent or educator overlooked, and the conference becomes a missed opportunity for real progress.

Opening the door to more frequent "conversations" rather than "conferences" within the mindset of an educator can minimize negative impacts and have potential alternative benefits, which include:

- Becoming more approachable.

- The inclusion of easier language for all.
- Each person involved (educator, student, and parent) can have a chance to participate in the conversation.
- Immediate feedback can be easier to receive (from a student and/or parent).

Natural Abilities are Furthered

"Conversations" rather than "conferences" facilitate an exchange of natural abilities and natural interactions to occur, both with the student and the parent.

Natural abilities of the student: A conversation and talking with a student, rather than lecturing, will result in less pressure, greater understanding, and an increased level of comfort and encouragement from the educator to the student to be felt and communicated.

Natural abilities of the parent: A conversation promotes a natural tone of desire for understanding, where a parent can become open to hearing and listening about their child's performance. Likewise, a conversation allows for the concerns of a parent to be heard and their goals, hopes, and focus points about their child to show in the conversation naturally. If a student is present during this conversation, they may also be more inclined to develop a greater interest or attention in their own performance, knowing their teacher and parents are on the same page.

Conversations and simply talking, although seemingly obvious, are sometimes overlooked. Often, the understood boundary between students and teachers and parents and teachers is maintained too far, interfering with essential communication.

TWO: Reveal the Truth – "Honesty *is* the Best Policy"

Tell the whole truth and nothing but the truth!

There should never be a reason for an educator to hide or not reveal a student's ability in the appropriate setting because that action defeats the purpose of guided growth, development, and learning.

The abilities of children and students always show whether those abilities are outstanding, above level, satisfactory, or need further assistance. To try to pass students or not communicate that a student needs additional attention in any area is a disservice to that child, their parents, and the learning process. If a student does not learn foundational elements and it is not communicated truthfully to parents, the parents may not be able to see for themselves the true measured skills of their child.

Additional support may be beyond the abilities of some educators and even school capacities. However, answering a question from parents, such as "How is my child doing in reading?" should not be overlooked by responding, "They are doing well," if that is really not the case.

Tests, quizzes, evaluations, exams, worksheets, and more are all tools for learning and measurement. When a pattern of consistent decline or a low plateau of understanding is identified, an educator now has the data from the results of those tools to reach deeper and understand why. It is also an obligation to tell the truth by communicating with the student and then, according to an institution's policy, either the administration, the parent, or both.

Unfortunately, some institutions, parents, and even other educators pressure educators to overlook student performance, resulting in a passing grade or even higher marks in grades. While this is sometimes meant with good intentions, it is a disservice to the student, as that student will not master the foundational elements that are necessary building blocks for success once in higher grade levels in the future. Any gaps intentionally or unintentionally overlooked will eventually show, and the student will again struggle.

A proactive approach to recognizing a student's actual needs in an honest way is part of the purpose of being an educator. To teach, we must assess to check for progress and ensure that learning occurs and the student shows growth. When a student needs additional help, a good educator becomes a great educator by investing effort and further attention in helping that child succeed with integrity for all.

THREE: Progressive Positive Discussion (PPD)

Is your "educator glass" half empty or half full? Hopefully, it will be half full and even overflowing, with a positive outlook on your role as an educator and the use of positive language to reflect this outlook. Encouragement comes from the messages and, more importantly, the ways and words in which these positive messages are crafted and communicated to both students and parents. The author of this book has created the method of *Progressive Positive Discussion* (PPD) to aid in communicating encouragement.

Progressive Positive Discussion (PPD) is defined as the method of ongoing communication that encourages credit for positive achievement based on positive craft and effective delivery of a message with stipulations removed.

The Craft and Structure of the Same Events Can Create Different Outcomes

There is a story that best exemplifies this method. A king called a man to come to interpret the king's dream. So, the king told the man about his dream. The man told the king that his dream meant that all the king's family would die before him. Upon hearing this, the king had the man killed. The king called upon another man. The man came, and the king told him about his dream. This man said to the king that the king would live the longest in his family. Upon hearing this meaning, the king was pleased and rewarded the man.

What was told to the king by both men was the same. Only the way the message was crafted through the words chosen by each man ultimately made each man meet his fate. This is the same type of situation that can happen in fundamental communication theories, whether it is one-way or two-way communication to a single person or millions of people at a time. The importance of crafting and delivering a message that educators communicate to students and parents determines how the message will be received. Awareness of saying something in the most positive way is the most productive way to achieve results.

The following is an example of PPD: How crafting positive words and delivery can lead to better encouragement and communication.

Situation One: A student has poor behavior; it is time to communicate this to the parent.

Don't say: "Your son/daughter is too disruptive and talkative in class."

Effect: By asserting that this one student is the only focus and cause of a problem, a parent might become immediately defensive, thus becoming unreceptive to receiving additional feedback about their child. Further, they could be turned away to discuss possible proactive solutions to prevent the student from engaging in poor behavior and focus the student toward a positive direction and overall outcome. The receiver of this negative message might also turn away from the purpose of communicating this message and divert (defensive technique) to another point or topic without resolving the main issue.

Say: "Your son/daughter would benefit from using their energy to speak in class at the appropriate times and will gain more from listening quietly to build comprehension when they are not participating."

Effect: Crafting the message into a positive suggestion based on an adverse action might leave the parent to ask a follow-up question of "how." Further suggestions can be made to direct the conversation towards an improvement plan immediately. Likewise, this crafting method will prevent the receiver (the parent) from becoming defensive, as the message is no longer the tone of a complaint but rather an observation about behavior, again allowing a positive approach to constructive feedback.

Removing the Stipulator: Don't Qualify the Positive; Leave the 'But' Behind

The idea of something good linked to something of concern is discouraging, and the good will not be remembered. The sayings of "no news is good news" and "bad news is always remembered" are true. Coupling good news with bad news has become a habit in communication to soften the blow of the bad news. Instead, this process only softens the effect of the positive praise and earned outcome of a positive effort and allows the good news to be forgotten the second the words "but," "however," or a stipulator is communicated.

The following is a typical example of how feedback is communicated to parents and even the administration about a student:

> *"This student works well with others, <u>but</u> he or she needs to improve his or her listening skills."*

The positive element has been tied to an area of focus and improvement and presented as a combined thought. The "good news" that the student "works well with others" is overshadowed by the stipulator "but." The concern that "he or she needs to improve his or her listening skills" is now the statement's focus, and the positive is no longer "newsworthy" or essential to communicate with the same weight.

Using PPD, let positive elements and areas of focus and improvement stand alone, each as a separate, independent statement.

Here is the same feedback, communicated using PPD, as **two separate statements**, removing the stipulator:

> *"This student works well with others, and their group cooperation is strong. An area that they need to focus on is listening to improve their understanding of the material."*

Two distinct, separate statements have been identified, and the positive part of the message, or "good news," does not exist based on the part of the message that includes areas of needed improvement or "bad news." Credit is given where the student deserves it, and recognition and encouragement have been communicated to the parent.

Always remember, no matter the method of communication (spoken in conversation or written as comments on a report card or progress report), let the positive stand alone. In an additional statement, without a stipulator such as "but," couple the area of focus with a positive strong suit of the student. Communicate and identify the truth of the need for improvement and use it to offer a method or plan of support to be discussed on an ongoing basis. This is the process of *Progressive Positive Discussion* (PPD).

Let one point help the other, not bring it down!

FOUR: Repetition of Expectations

Educators repeat and remind as much as they communicate greetings to students and parents. While repetition may seem tiring and full of lackluster, it is essential. The method in which repetition occurs can bring the sparkle back into the message, process, and outcome, bringing greater encouragement for all.

Remind both students and parents of expectations. The more mindsets and visions are shared, and the goals and focus are clearly identified, the more the repetition of those goals becomes their own words of encouragement.

Take, for example, the story of *The Little Engine That Could*. Each time the engine struggled to chug further on the tracks, it would repeat, "I think I can, I think I can, I think I can." This repetition helped the engine recall his task, remind him of its purpose and expectations, and use his own words of encouragement to achieve his goal.

Repetition for Students

Even in one 30-minute class, students can be told what to do once every three to five minutes, ranging from repeating directions to repeating the exact words of warnings and requesting students to adjust their behavior. This can be challenging.

When repetition has negative results, such as a loss of interest and attention to what is being said, it becomes essential to repeat expectations in different ways.

The following steps of repetition can help reinforce expectations:

1. Ask students what expectations are.
2. Repeat what they say and ask if they are on the right path for those expectations.
3. Correct and clarify the answer to repeat what the expectations are.

This interactive approach can get an individual or a group back on track through students helping each other because they identify and encourage other students who are off track in the first two steps. The third step allows the educator to regain the lead and control of the class and reset for a statement of encouragement to be made while repeating and finalizing the expectations.

Repetition for Parents

For parents, encouragement can be repeated in immediate and long-term ways, ranging from conversations to weekly or monthly newsletters or progress reports sent home or posted online.

In conversational communication, the primary purpose is to discuss a student's progress, which can be initiated by stating a positive point about the student.

For example:

> *"In reading, this student can find the main ideas of a story very well."*

To build a more comprehensive discussion, *include the positive element before the areas of improvement and focus are included* (as outlined in Chapter 3, "Progressive Positive Discussion"). **Repeat the expectations** while communicating feedback to lead to a plan of action.

For example:

> *"In reading, this student can find the main ideas of a story very well. They sometimes have trouble learning new vocabulary words. If they can work from now until the end of the quarter on learning word meanings from what they can identify in the main ideas of passages, they should be able to improve their vocabulary words overall."*

When used to connect a strong area of learning to help a weaker area of learning, the repetition of strong and weak points is more encouraging, logical, and strategic. This way of repetition can also be used to inform a parent about the current abilities, growth, and potential growth of their child. Likewise, a sense of timeline with a goal further makes words of encouragement into words of reality and a plan of action.

FIVE: *Be* the Encouragement!

Students notice everything! And to repeat it (for good humor), students notice everything about YOU as the educator! Students notice everything, whether in a bad mood, one minute late to class on Wednesday, or even if you use a new pen to write with!

When children are with educators for up to eight hours daily, familiarity sets in from both sides. As students and parents become familiar, understandings, expectations, and assumptions can become part of the relationship.

Developing a certain expectation as a teacher about a particular student (negative or positive) is a slippery slope that should be avoided, as it will detract from an overall encouraging mindset. Any predetermined mindset, even based on repetitive behavior and outcomes, should always be avoided because it will detract from encouraging communication!

Many teachers can anticipate the students who will get a high or low score before an assignment or test is handed out. A preconceived thought shifts an entire perspective, sense of mood, and, more importantly, how you are identified, perceived, and felt by your students. Just as much as students judge each other, they judge us, educators, right back, even if they never seem to show it. Therefore, as educators, we should set and be the example and remove our judgment, as it will only place our ability to educate and encourage into a box of pessimistic restriction. Once that box is established within us, consciously or not, an internal shift can occur, causing a loss of interest, energy, and a place where the true qualities of a great, trusted, and devoted educator would be lost.

Entering a classroom with a frown, no greeting, or going straight to the desk to sit down before a spoken word does not *show* encouragement.

Imagine attending an exercise class where the instructor sits the whole time and only gives a vague task at the start. Then, a few minutes into the class, the instructor begins to eat and text for the rest of the time. You might immediately leave, try to complain, stay and work quietly until it is over while being disappointed, or do something to get the instructor's attention (who is *showing* they really couldn't care less if you are there or not).

These are the same outcomes that students might display if they do not feel that their instructor is encouraging.

Take a moment to set a positive mood and tone so that students can feel the learning experience come to life. Present information where at least one student asks a follow-up question. Praise a student who gave a correct answer or even went slightly off-topic but showed effort and a connection to that topic to expand and participate.

Likewise, appreciate parents who take the time to ask any question about their child. They are taking an interest and making an effort to be involved and cultivate encouragement and support for learning at home.

Be the encouragement to make each class count as an opportunity to enrich a young mind and understand something new, even if it is about an "unplanned" topic. Be the encouragement so students feel encouraged to think critically, learn, and come back for more!

Personal Contract for Encouragement

I, _____, promise to challenge myself to uphold the elements of positive encouragement in my communication to students, parents, and the community I serve.

Three immediate changes I will make to encourage communication:

1.

2.

3.

Three long-term changes that I will plan to implement towards encouraging communication:

1.

2.

3.

I will work to the best of my ability and stay encouraged to maintain my positive encouragement to others!

Optional witness: _____

Date: _____

About the Author

Dr. Alexandra V. Maragha is an educator, researcher, and journalist with over 10 years of combined experience. She holds a Ph.D. in Islamic Sciences. She also holds a Master of Science degree in Curriculum and Instruction and graduated summa cum laude with her bachelor's degree in communication and journalism. She has designed curriculum and instruction courses and methodologies and has taught in elementary, secondary, and adult education settings. Her research on instructional communication, the communication of Prophet Mohammad (PBUH), and the development of an instructional model based on the Sunnah of Prophet Mohammad (PBUH) have been presented at international research conferences and published in international academic journals. Her expertise in communicative theory, messaging, and instructional design has merged the fields of education and communication to contribute to necessary research to enhance instructional communication in educational settings.

> *"While 'the medium is the message,' as defined by communicative theorist Marshall McLuhan, it must be understood and implemented in educational settings. Educators must be aware that how they teach affects what they teach and, in turn, how students learn. Communicating learning must be realized, crafted, and delivered most consciously and beneficially to improve learning potential to reach ultimate results."*
>
> -Dr. Alexandra V. Maragha

Dr. Maragha has also served as editor for various publications, reviewer for academic journals, and has written numerous articles for multiple international news outlets, focusing on politics and global affairs. Dr. Maragha continues to conduct research in related fields and education and implement instruction within educational settings.

www.ingramcontent.com/pod-product-compliance
Lightning Source LLC
Chambersburg PA
CBHW061317040426
42444CB00010B/2688